The Fiction of Stone

The Fiction of Stone

Barb Lundy

The New Atlantian Library

THE NEW ATLANTIAN LIBRARY
Is an imprint of
ABSOLUTELY AMAZING eBOOKS

Published by Whiz Bang LLC, 926 Truman Avenue, Key West, Florida 33040, USA.

ISBN 978-1-951150-82-2

For information contact:
Publisher@AbsolutelyAmazingEbooks.com

Dedicated to poet Lois Beebe Hayna. You are missed.

The Fiction of Stone

TABLE OF CONTENTS

ONE

TWO

THREE

A Gleaning
The Marriage Divination
Unguarded
Predictions in a Dry Wind
At the Great Divide
Friday After Five
At Avebury
Inductions
Reverie
The Fugitive
The Fifth String
Passing By
Amati
Eddy Street
The Disposition
At the Road Show
Bed Near the Window
2:00 AM
Conversion Chart
Before the Frost
The Mastermind
The Disappearance

FOUR

ONE

Fantasy is probably the oldest literary device
for talking about reality.

-Ursula K. Le Guin

Barb Lundy

PROFILE

van Gogh by Toulouse-Lautrec

My hand records far more than I see.
This late afternoon Vincent sits
alone in a corner of the
Tambourin Cafe. I set out
cardboard, pen and chalk.

Air coils around him. White light
bleaches his red beard
starches blue wall shadows.
Ginger eyes often reflect liquid terror
but today I capture impenetrability.

The steam of dying rises from inert
arms. In stark contrasts, with rotating
rhythms, I assume the raw
convulsions of his brush. Sketch
reckless lines. Use bold suffusions of

sulfurs, malachite and cyanics. Dusk
devours my view as I rough in a glass
of absinthe. Vincent, leaning on
brittle steps, drifts into the
darkfall, a man already forgotten.

At the Lapidary

This scrap of amber holds
the quill and crest of a
feather from the
belly of a water fowl
that flew a million
years ago.

A feather that settled at the base
of a hymenaea tree
and soaked into the
sweat of its sap.

This stone still hums
the song of extinct birds
carries the breeze
and the heat of
ancient afternoons
and keeps company
with veins of crystal.

Barb Lundy

Of Confidences

Talent carries her
beyond the river front that
spans rows of two story flats
receptionist jobs and steady income men.

Faces come alive beneath her inventive brush.
Glaze intensifies a violet eye.
She lifts a brow to disclose raw aspiration
turns a lip to hint displeasure.

Early mornings offer the best light.
Sun sweeps her canvases
to give rise to a chaos
lost to muted masks of late day hours.

Across-the-water confessions fill her gallery.
Her portraits reveal. Admit.
Request no absolution.
No oath seals what she sees.

Breathing Spell

As the universe breathes out, then in
stars and planets tilt and spin
until the space between them begins
to pull deep and wide
to transform to a billion-years-from-now sky
to pattern constellations that do not coincide
with our galaxies.

And what if we could choose
ex and in halations? What if we refused
to stand against unnerving news
to bend to the uncut exhaustion of days
that twist to vacuous cliché?
Would we stay and fill
our lungs with ease
or would escape tease away
our will to breathe?

Barb Lundy

FALL FROM GRACE

Actually, it was more of a spill from grace
a slow tumble
a slumping descent
a collapse best
calculated by
over-the-shoulder glances.

As with any decline worth mentioning
it involved a degree of
moral decay,
though her understanding
of moral shifted
from year to year.

The pacts she'd made with herself
remained secret. No one else
detected declining
expectations,
the slow extinction
of trust.

She leans down to regain agility,
realizes the worst kind of grace
to fall from is her own.

The Gathering

Returning
they revive the ancient
language of youth
though cadence falters
and inflections flatten.
Words slow
for edits
before they reach air.

Returning
they ring oblong linened tables
lean in to listen
to who's doing what where.
Their eyes
tell the untold
in glances latticed with
decades lived apart.

Returning
they lull to vague reminiscence.
Memories spare in detail
allow a sting of
sadness at parting.
They relish mingling with interstate
strangers they don't have to
pretend to know.

Barb Lundy

Chihuahua After Sunset

Cereus spine masquerade as dead
twigs snagged in desert shrub.
Dry between the summer storms that
coax temporary conversions.

Cactus buds swell among thorns.
Enchantment coils stems until white
petals open to moon shadows.
Spice dark arid breeze.

Dare to walk as sand shudders alive
with sidewinder and wind scorpion.
Queen-of-the-Night flowers bloom once
in a season. Resist the temptation
to transplant impetuous petals.

When Building a Bridge

Scan the landscape for two opposing
points that request connection.

Imagine who will begin or
end a journey on its span.

Understand the temperament of early
spring run-offs and flash floods.

Calculate the speed and weight
of adventure and escape.

Remember bridges suspend certainty.
tempt us to walk on air.

Barb Lundy

HANDSOME AND THE HAG

One day fairy tales will no longer drone
stories fueled by testosterone
their toad princes archaic sine-qua-nons.

That willowy beauty, her gnarled beast,
or opera's phantom and damsel sweet
now characters who no longer meet.

Instead, let's script handsome and his hag.
Join his tight abs with her saddlebags.
Let them stroll into sunsets with a swag.

You can't imagine this affair?
You think it's more than splitting hairs?
This subtle shift a daring dare?

Once written it spins all rendezvous.
Each child who listens makes it come true.
This fairytale that can happen to you.

KEEP THE MUSIC GOING

He pulls a soft low voice
from the throat of his trumpet,
sounds swell to urgency.

The floor shudders. Piano keys
mimic a high pitched wail then
spiral down to throbbing flats.

His trumpet speaks languages
born of Fats and Ella. Of
corner bar jam sessions.

He plays to hear himself speak
to face locked-down fear
to keep the music going.

Barb Lundy

THE EXCHANGE

Just now, as his thoughts slip
onto air and gain velocity
she interprets the syllables
with a shrug of her shoulder
with flat return tones
and a disarming stare.

He can’t reel the words back.
Can’t disassemble and reconstruct
until they fit together with
flawless precision.
His draft ideas transform
to indelible memory.

Hers.

REVISIONS

Long before he evaporated from the
inside out, before he tangled words,
before he returned at noon
from evening lectures,
he confused her name with mine.

First she stifled chance caresses,
hollowed our laughter.
Then, with seeping
deliquescence,
she lightened my bed.

We scattered his ashes at Anasazi ruins.
He knew them better than any of us,
even her. She came.
We stood apart, tethered by
betrayal. His.

Afternoon clouds crowd the mountains.
Hold little for my parched
kaffir lilies. Rain withers to low
hanging heat in the
vespertine hours of August.

Barb Lundy

OFF CANYON ROAD

The few walls that room this space
hold up draft sketches,
carry current and detour wind.

Her fingers play keys
to ink thoughts,
to cast sound.

A beige stuffed chair
and ottoman
curl her into books.

Time ticks in high windows.
Cycle shadow, blinding sun
and the sweeping solace of stars.

THE MAH JONGG WOMEN

Talk of bamboos and dead walls
turns to kids grown and gone
and random mentions of husbands.
After a game she often joins them
under the wide stretch of maples.

Words flow in waves across the table.
She stays on the edges of conversations
sure they think it odd she never married
or had children. Now she lives a life she
didn't choose and can't change.

They invite her to too-hot-to-cook barbeques.
Tempt her to try a round of their diversion
but she doesn't like games.
Life is hard enough. She played
by the rules and it didn't work.

The Mah Jongg women see possibility in
every hand. Apply strategy. Lean on luck.
They let go of winds before dragons or flowers.
Know the difficulty of finding pairs.
Gamble on every tile they pass.

Barb Lundy

URGENT THIRSTS FORGOTTEN

This valley of husked crops
of high tasseled weeds
of deep dust and impassive soil

checkers to sun and shadow
when slate clouds clear the mountains.
Electricity sears wild packets of air.

Expectation pools in plowed trenches.
Dried earth begins to yield as clouds depart
before deep roots have a chance to drink.

WITHOUT THE DEPOT OR THE TRAIN

Consider banishing the mysterious fog
surrounding her arrival.
Dispel iced air swirling
to embrace chance meetings.
Anna Karenina's first scene, minus the
train whistle wailing and wheels
screeching to a stop
falls flat.

Had Anna called Vronsky
by his first name from the start
she might have paired her two Alexeis'.
Together, passion and calm composure
make one tolerable lover.

Instead Tolstoy pens a
predictable end. Guilt, revenge
and reckless daring merge
to the suicide price
nervy women tediously pay.
Anna throws herself beneath a train
at the only-way-out depot
where it all began.

Barb Lundy

THE APPRENTICE

At the gloaming, the branches of
a Hawthorne shield him
from a growing audience.
He checks the inside pockets
of his left sleeve.

He licks his lips as he watches
a doddering woman and her
svelte daughter settle on tree
trunk seats. I catch him
in this private reverie.

Contempt gleams from beneath his
auburn brows. Dullards, he rasps
as he secretes the glimmering dust
I offer. Seconds later
he makes a sweeping entrance.

He throws my mix into the fire and
exploding light dazzles the crowd.
Mocking imprints every sleight-of-hand.
Fleer and flourish mark his bow. He hides
a curling lip against their frantic clapping.

WILDFIRE

When the devouring begins
when blaze eats oak and blue spruce
when yellow iceland poppies flash to ash the
feast is held on arbitrary acres.

The ember from a campfire
the slice of a lightning strike
sets the siege in motion
lead by the impulse of wind.

Resistance becomes a feeble pledge.
Thunderheads and the river course
force the burn to a random end.
The flames die without ever looking back.

Barb Lundy

THE GRAVEL MAKER

She pounds
stones harvested near spider lilies on the beach,
stones hidden in the ferns beneath lancewoods,
stones that tell their interiors at the touch
of her questioning palm.

She pounds
heavy stones, dug out, then pushed and dragged,
stones she leaned into her hip to carry,
stones that swell to a cairn guarding her chair
under the almond tree, in front of her house.

She pounds
stones into rocks and rocks into pebbles, and
pebbles into crumbs of pebbles. Scarred fingers
cup raw fragments. She pitches them into a heap
that puddles, piles, then pyramids.

She pounds
with a hammerhead driven by her right arm.
The dust of transformation swirls around her.

Settles on her eyelids, between her toes. She
strikes fragility and shatters the fiction of stone.

TWO

Doubt is longwinded, certainty brief.

-Mason Cooley

Barb Lundy

VANISHING ACT

I cannot find my car or the keys to it
so I no longer travel as I once did
to tennis matches
to mountain outcroppings
that told me stories
of having lived beneath seas
or to the ports where we
boarded ships that
carried us around the globe.

I cannot find my study or the view from its window
where I played with equations
to tempt my students to question.
Lost too is the room where I rested
my cheek in the easy curve
of his shoulder
and the yard where daughters
cart wheeled across grass.

I stored every odd sized parcel
of knowing into memory
a reserve given to evaporation over time.
Tonight I sip open fire coffee
listen to wind spin off the canyon floor
watch stars glance up at me from
a river running the raven night.
Light slides current fast past my campsite.

AND AGAIN

Cured stiff by sweat, the electric
blue costume begins to bend.
She stretches, touches the wooden floor
that pulses with the beat of feet,
vibrates music from the pit.

She sails on rings of air
that twist and stretch, takes the
swing of her weight
wide and up through space
before her luxuriant unwinding.

Each vault demands complete attention.
Perfection may come in a lighter lift
An invisible landing.
After a long deep breath
she begins. Again.

Barb Lundy

THE DIG

If you see reproach in
my unblinking stare know
the midday sun empties
sockets of shadow.
Could you look into the
blue black of my eyes
you'd erase your green
calculations about my
age or my homeland.

You scrawl notes about cultural
burial patterns based on the
angle of my petrified limbs.
That afternoon
I slipped on a wet rock
and landed in a dead sprawl
at the bottom of the ravine.
My son flew from my arms.

When you find him, will you
ascribe sacrificial import?
For now inhale my dust.
Let it cling to the moist underside
of your tongue. Each particle
narrates my lifetime. Depart with
bone fragments, heady conclusions
and an unaccountable
fear of falling.

COASTING

We plot navigational charts before
shoving off. He opens a binnacle
custom built for his small boat.
Checks and rechecks calculations.

Shore steadies his course. I prefer
an isotropic view and settle in open water.
Read gull swoops and the day star,
alert to danger in every breeze.

We each inhale rogue winds,
chase apparitions, scan clotted mists.
We each double points in search
of erratic ventriloquist cries.

Chaos excites me, while he grows
a manic confusion. We anchor at sunset.
Weigh our words to circumvent the most
treacherous rip tides of the day.

Barb Lundy

ALL THE RAGE

The fashion retrospective
features brass collar bands
piled high to stretch necks.
Feature devices to push up and
pull down parts.
Our guide provides
testimonial to the
rib crushing corsets by
winnowing her own waist
to a grotesque seventeen inches.

Skirts, bustled and hooped, require
contortionist drills.
Men sport padded calves.
Ghostly x-rays
chronicle the torture
of the three inch lotus slipper.
In every century
chic refinement renders
daily confinement.

ABIQUIU

This canyon cut flat tablelands.
A stream spirals deep
through red clay and rock.

Illusion melds with matter here.
An unexpected red wildflower
perches on bleached stone.

She watches a hawk glide the cerulean sky.
Each dive, each rise
provokes an ache of envy.

Barb Lundy

JAMMED

Do you know a decent locksmith?
I've exhausted the yellow pages.
Referrals from friends fizzled. Those who
do come shake their heads and leave.

This is not the brightest professional lot.
They hawk expensive security systems
while demonstrating with each twist of their
precision tools, the hoax of impregnability.

I explain I don't need them to jimmy a door to
reveal what I know is already behind it, or crack
a lock box when I hold the entire contents list in
my hand. What skill is there in that?

I want a key, that upon turning, shapes the amorphous
and sculpts the diffuse. Certainly it has been
invented by now. If you know someone who
can get the job done, give me a call.

RUINS AT THE IONIAN SEA

Stone steps gleam chalk white at noon
scrubbed by winds that carry
the salt of the sea.
They lead to a ledge
stretching the reach of a wall
that overlooks
slate and teal waves
and nothing more.

Stay until the twilight gathers.
Lean shadows fatten
with the casualties
of accumulated days.
Stay as long as the
light allows retreat
and can still
point the way down.

Barb Lundy

LEGACIES

The three women,
grandmother, mother and daughter,
tempt the appetite
help the deserving
get things done the right way.

And in each woman
a hard-wired anger triggers
long silences
cutting observations
and the banging of pots.

The rest of the family
calculate potential conflicts and
angle outside her anxieties. Hope the
curse of perpetually feeling
second-best recedes to extinction.

JAR OF BRUSHES

Brushes lean, bristle up, inside the jar,
shimmering brushes linger in the jar,
reminding me I've yet to take them far.
Even sleek sable brushes cannot find,
in lines both bold and timid cannot find,
the water lilies bursting in my mind.
Older brushes, speckled, sometimes stiff,
stroked colored angles clumsy, crude and stiff.
One Saturday I tossed them in a tiff.
New brushes speak in whispers as I pass,
rustle, jeer and taunt me as I pass,
Perhaps, I say out loud, I'll take a class.
The impulse speeds through, doesn't stay,
I push the jar of brushes out of my way.

Barb Lundy

RECITAL

The moon attends my dark concert
peers from a balcony window
fills the room with
curious shadow. Memories
open then close with
a surge of arpeggios.

Hands perform blind rituals
on the innocence of ivory
glide on lacquered sheens.
Fuse thin descants with
strikes of dissonance. Await
the stir to compose.

Too soon, the murky blues
of morning shroud the
radiant face. Retreat from
the raw reach of dawn.
I stop playing
to an empty house.

A PUZZLE

If he planned this arrival
no map or itinerary
remains to jog his memory.

From any vantage point
border crossings dissolve
to arcadia, to notion.

Indelible acid imprints
the passport
sewn beneath his skin.

Double helix chains hold
the key to an identity
he decodes over decades.

And he departs as he came
in the dim of dream
to another random destination.

Barb Lundy

FORECLOSURE

Crates of books stack against
family room furniture
bubble wrapped paintings and
redwood planters emptied of earth.

She wakes at 3 a.m.
Stares from the window at a
scene soon lost. Listens
to the runoff rush of the creek.

Returns to the stacks of letters
written in his kinetic hand
to bent and yellowed leaflets
that retrace their nomadic years.

He coughs and turns slightly in
fitful sleep. Rest replenishes little
when it seeps from night into day.
Dissolves to confinement.

She swallows down the pyrosis of
rising panic. Separates need from
small indulgences. Finds the limits
of a cardboard box infuriating.

THE POSSIBLE BROTHER-IN-LAW

Sis says he's her second chance at love
this man of soliloquied clichés.
He never lets on that he notices
when we try to get a word in.

This holiday we orchestrated a schedule
of feigned attention. Tag-teamed in fifteen
minute intervals, pretending to follow the
yo-yo monotony of his high whine.

He delivers a script about his laissez-faire boss
about nearing his breaking point
about reading the handwriting on the wall
about co-workers who cast aspersions.

Sis has absorbed his penchant for platitude.
They even fight in bromides.
After breakfast this morning she accused
him of being all talk and no action.

Barb Lundy

SIDELONG

In stolen sleep
she sees
clouds bursting,
feels exploding rain
on her face, and
stretches out her hands
to snatch
wide drops.
A red sky fades to
peach then to the sheen of
ripe blackberries.
Double winged
crickets sing
to fireflies
until they spin
dizzying lights.

Waking, she longs for the
knowing of
days when
her feet
never left an
imprint in the grass,
when steps
never meaning to go
anywhere,
took her where she
wanted to go.

Now she follows
directions so
routine, she
arrives at places she
never meant
to find.

Barb Lundy

STANDING APPOINTMENT

Eyes closed against the light
he relaxes as she snaps the
plastic cloak around his collar
guides his head back with ease.

He leans into the massage of
wash and rinse and wash again
enjoys the quick wrap of a warm towel
and the long strokes of the comb.

Her hands pull strands of hair tight.
She clicks scissors against the tension.
Moves methodically from top to side.
Her fingers tousle for form.

In the sweep of the brush
the precision final trim
he admits his hunger for touch.
Vows to keep his hair short.

CHILD'S PLAY

Her breath shallows
when his key turns
when hinges sigh under
the weight of listing oak.

And when he shuts the door
everyone tiptoes
on the thin black ice
of his silent rage.

She waits in a corner
of the den until
Budweiser and ESPN
lull him to sleep.

Then she drops captured
cat spiders in his hair
and watches as they
crawl awake his terror.

Barb Lundy

MONODY

You can't get stoned on incense.
This high sweet scent doesn't come from
college days. It makes more miserable the
collected memories that fill the pews.

I rerun our decades-long talks about being
single women without children.
We are, or were, the only two in our
crowd not to graduate to families.

They drone on at the alter. Call you a
sinner and ask that you be forgiven.
If you could, you'd get up and leave
even with your mother sitting up front.

Fear cloisters me. You become another
character to exit the drama of my days.
Destinations loom empty of faces.
Calendars clear. The phone quiets.

I feel guilty weighing my private desolation
against your abbreviated days. They walk
your casket out the door waving censors.
Incense inspires the surreal after all.

SKINNED ALIVE

Because the nose job from her
Grandmother was a graduation gift
she dared not refuse it
though she still breathes through
flared nostrils no one sees.

Her fiancé suggested liposuction to fit
into his great aunt's handmade
Scottish lace gown worn by
his mother on her wedding day.
Her winnowed waist lasted a year.

The kids helped her dig out thistles the
afternoon she stumbled over a
flagstone and implanted the gardening
trowel in her chin. During reconstruction
the surgeon added a free nip and tuck.

After the divorce, the career counselor
advised an eye lift and a botox blast.
Her too thin lips broke into a smile.
She couldn't find her calendar
for a follow-up appointment.

Barb Lundy

THREADING THE MOJAVE

Sunset widen to coral, to
fired orange above cacti that
cluster near red boulders.
This desert cross-stitch kit
promises retreat.

She safety pins loose buttons.
Hems with two-way tape
sutures xxx of tinted floss
to edge a playa lake. To shape
a distant mountain.

In the scene's quiet she senses a
blacktail rattler under the brush,
a tarantula tunneling out.
She pencils action into the
chimerical solitude.

THE PROPOSAL

They take a break near towering blue spruce.
Listen to spring runoff spill over the rock bed
watch the sun gleam in wide splashes that
arch cold sprays over the embankment.

He takes her off guard when he kneels.

The adventure appeals to her.
If the past gives a glimpse into the future
she knows delaying tactics paralyze, that
taking risks pays off.

He studies her face.

Assumptions offer dangers too. She thinks
she knows what she is getting into yet
worries reality often falls short. Despite
doubts she decides to says yes.

He ties his boot. What sounds better, Mexican or Thai?

Barb Lundy

AT THE CEMETERY

I travel the wrong road to your grave.
Convenience placed your headstone
among the neat rows at Andersonville
though you wanted Arlington.
Mother decided it.

The collective years of my life
now exceed your own and I am left
as I am every visit
to weigh acceptance against excuse
and man against father.

Sunlight warms the top of my head
as it did the days you promised
time together. Light fades to dusk
as it did then, until sleep
claims me from waiting.

Had I grasped the cost of killing
in your eyes, I might have
understood your absences.
Interpreted shots of scotch as so many
short seasons from memory.

Everything sweats in July in Georgia,
even stone. I trace your name with
fingertips calloused by chance.
Next year I'll go to Arlington and
cast your violets to the breeze.

THE SWAP

You trade a Lauren sweater
for my hazel twig amulets
that secure safe journeys.
Barter Broadway tickets
for moonsilvered coins
to lure a soul mate.

We both believe in magic.
You bank on the imagined
I attract what I need.

As you swing a pendulum
over maps, over photos
of unsuspecting men,
I settle into center seats
wearing the plush plum warmth
of someone willing to shape fate.

Barb Lundy

AS A WOMAN

I carry night deep in my eyes
the dark night that excites
light

The singing night that hums
hypnotic day's sun
down

The long night that lingers
casually speaking
stars

The wary night that trembles
warns mist-at-midnight
terror.

As a woman I walk within
my eyes, through captured
constellations.

And outside my door,
beyond memory, this night
beckons.

Three

The truth is rarely pure and never simple.

-Oscar Wilde

Barb Lundy

A GLEANING

Ancient Egypt recognized three seasons

Born in akhet, the season of inundation
under skies shrouded by clouds
I don't know how to walk
free of the land.
My toes dig into the slick stick of mud
and I pull the weight of ground
on my journeys.

Born before peret, the season of sowing
the season when strong earth
receives seed, I miss the
incense of just opened soil
of walking between rows
furrowed and tilled
readied for bulbs and cuttings.

Born before shemu, the season of growing,
season of bees and of worms,
I walk past wheat stalks and branches
bowed with berries. Until a ritual of
tongue and teeth appears in dream
until I wake to gilt sunrise
until I pull and pick to reap my first harvest.

THE MARRIAGE DIVINATION

Maggel retrieves a crisp apple in the dunking.
I emerge with drenched hair and dodge
the questioning eye of the priest. Hallowtide
denies me marriage for a third year.

We fatten cold torches in the great fire at the
eleventh hour. Carry flickering fortune back to
home hearths, scanning shrouded paths.
They say the dead masquerade this night.

I don't believe spirits roam the hillside, but they
can slip into dreams. We dare not close our
eyes against the dark. Maggel raids dried plums, I
grab hazel nuts left for phantom intruders.

The Druid limps over the knoll at dawn. Smiles at
Maggel, the soon-to-be-bride and frowns at me.
Believing in his magic, he never guesses
I just keep my mouth shut under water.

Barb Lundy

UNGUARDED

I catch the stranger's glance as I pass the
hallway mirror. Startled, her azure
eyes watch me, cool. Cold? Gentian
specks stare leaden. Opaque? I retreat

to the tangled remains of last year's
garden, underbrush to frosted heather
rising above fragile hyacinth.
Too soon, I clip the early blossoms.

Arrange them in the crystal vase beneath
reflection. Stand new growth against intrusion.
Look again, and greet her chilling candor. No trace
of an unfinished future lingers in her eyes

PREDICTION IN DRY WIND

First he noticed an unraveling of phrase
an economy of words and tighter tone
a holding back in small and subtle ways
and her need to spend more time alone.
Had he acted when the signs she gave were small
had he asked what force began to pull her back,
storm clouds may have passed, a short rainfall
but asking meant she'd answer and react.
So one month ran on to months and silence grew
and the language that they shared fell out of use.
Each forged paths that took them somewhere new
and each kept the terms of their unspoken truce.
An insulated ache stirs when he finds
some insignificant thing she left behind.

Barb Lundy

AT THE GREAT DIVIDE

Aspen argue in October. Their knobbed
elbows and bone white fingers point
conflicting directions. She roams the
naked grove. The promise of a meadow fills
her pocket. She lines the creases of her
palm with hard brown seeds.

Blows larkspur, rose crown and
scarlet paintbrush onto the crisp
afternoon breeze. Watches as they
sow in a thatch of bleached
spruce needles, parchment leaves
and the fine ash of late summer fires.

Shade, then shadows wrap the crest of the
Rocky Mountains. She understands the
power of demarcation. Last year she planted
patio geraniums in narrow boxes above
traffic. Now, making meadows with the
wave of her hand, she grows wild.

FRIDAY AFTER FIVE

She slips her jacket onto a cedar hanger
her silk blouse into the cleaning bag
hangs navy linen pants for another wearing
and frees toes from suntan hose.

Returns rings and earrings to velvet drawers
Makeup surrenders to clear clean water,
to lotion massaged into lids of tired eyes.
Brush strokes sweep away the day's tangles.

In her cotton nightshirt, she sprawls on the floor.
Takes deep breaths, exhales tedium and the absurd.
Waits to see if this ritual weekend resuscitation
will restore her to consciousness.

Barb Lundy

AT AVEBURY

Hulking stones stand
in circle fragments.
Biting mists sleek ancient
pockmarks smooth.
Rites gone to seed.

The daring speak for gods
or claim divinity.
Most people squint against
the brief lucidity of sun
and scan stars to augur purpose.

So tentative this navigation
between amnesia and
the vanishing point
we carve statues and arrange
stones. Scared sacred.

INDUCTIONS

She requests roses in her 20s.
Vases filled with perfect
red petals, predictable scents.

The baby years inspire sunflowers
Larger than life, overarching
the garden, living into October.

Lilies tempt as her teen turns 20.
More durable than her marriage
day lilies thrive in adverse soil.

In the sixth decade- wildflowers.
Never to be picked, peeking between
rocks, thriving in deserts. Untamed.

Barb Lundy

REVERIE

She doesn't remember the birth
of her child.
Not the details.
The feel of her son in her arms
the touch of his hand
the pull of his mouth on her nipple
decades ago.

Another night replays without warning.
She walks the park with a man she
hasn't seen in years. A breeze carries the
scent of just cut grass as she leans
against his shoulder. Follows the
angle of his hand to
find the swan, the eagle
and the great bear in a radiant sky.

Rogue memories revive raw longing
detonate tears. She attempts to believe
uncertainty curates the past
chance drafts the future.
Only now, only now she repeats.
The mantra fails to lighten her steps.

THE FUGITIVE

Early August hours slowly steep
clouds in vapored light.
Below his window the stream
swells then stills to satin.

Wisteria, white oaks and green
shutters slide seamlessly
from landscape to water in the
long brush strokes of dawn.

Hints of the hill garden fill the air.
Dew clings to toad lilies, lacquers
grass and clover that chill
the soles of his bare feet.

He despises the haughty gaze of
high-noon. Disappears when her
glinting eye dispels shadow
leaves nothing to imagination.

With knife and spoke shave he shapes
spindles behind half drawn shades.
Ventures out when dusk begins to
shimmer as it sips the last drops of sun.

Barb Lundy

THE FIFTH STRING

brought them together
Vivaldi, beneath his bow
weakened her knees.

He found his foot tapping
as she fiddled Murray's Reel
or The Red Hair Boy

They never learned to
merge their styles
or to play in harmony.

The reels became redundant
The classical stuffy
The fifth string their undoing.

PASSING BY

At the old carpenter's shed
shoes sit on the bottom step
thick soled
suede darkened by
woodland clay.
Leather ties slump
over heels worn slant.

On steps overgrown with weeds
a chic backless sandal
falls on its side
near the weathered door.
Its glossy brass buckles
catch the sun
One sandal. Nothing more.

And beneath a smudged
window pushed half way up
muslin curtains spin
out and then in
keep pace with a
late west afternoon wind
as toes play toe-to-toe within.

Barb Lundy

AMATI

He pulls a prop as I hold his violin.
Within its curves come echoes of the songs
that hum the grief of early trouvers
their soundless notes swell tenuous and long.
Too soon the quartet settles to begin.
He takes it back and opens up his score
tests one last string among the tuning din
then curtains move and silence is restored.
A frottola begins its easy sound
held by air and the bending of a bow.
Measures rise, release and soon rebound.
I listen but am carried past the flow.
Aware that long after we disband
these Amati songs will haunt my hands.

EDDY STREET

The aunts interrogate at Sunday
dinner. They circle the table
topped with a plywood plank
to fit in husbands and children.
It takes two second best linens
to cover the distance.

Will you have another slice of turkey?
Take a Parker House roll before
they get cold. Did you see we have
two wakes this Tuesday? And
All Saints is as far as you can get
from Our Lady of Angels.

They retreat with leftovers. Questions
simmer above soaking rose china and
the rip of cheesecloth sized to wrap
cloved ham. Can you imagine? Won't
tongues fly now. And what about
those McGillicuddy sisters?

What kind of woman wants
to be a judge? Those Your Honors
never lifting a finger to help.
No man'll have them.
Then again, they might just
have the ticket.

Barb Lundy

THE DISPOSITION

After years of ritual teas in the front room
she stands among Aunt Althea's
out-of-view memories
and decides which closets to sort.
Folds frayed lingerie
deciphers faded ink on saved cards.
Reduces Althea's life to
Goodwill
yard sale
take home
and toss
piles.

She separates a mound of drab chains
twisted beads and fat floral earrings.
Pulls out a ring from the jumble.
Finds amethyst under dust
volute silver under tarnish.
Slides it on her finger and
hears a wisp of laughter
ripple the room
as the stone catches sun.

AT THE ROAD SHOW

You have a marvelous piece done
quite near the end of her life.
Clean lines form an abstract of late
season leaves that fade from apricot to
jasmine then spill to intense ambers.

When I hold the vase near the light you can see
fragile patterns merge in a sheer, very nearly
brittle glass overlay. She quit the
states in her 60s for a town outside of
Paris and began experimenting.

She infused layers of color with movement.
One wonders if she flung a molten mesh into wind.
A splendid museum find, though she
insisted her created art for use. Fill it with
fresh cut flowers after you appraise. Insure.

Barb Lundy

BED NEAR THE WINDOW

The dazzle in his eyes
washes back when she arrives.
A smile
a nod
everything there but the impromptu
light offered others.

What she did is lost to
her or never known.
Old hurts find a way
to condemn even when
they fade from memory.

She longs for a
shriving pew
for a list of rote repentances that
add up to forgiveness.
Takes his frail hand in hers
holds it against
ghost failings.
He pulls away.
Slips to sleep.

2:00 AM

They exchange one last slow motion kiss
and begin to yield to sleep
when she whispers the words.
The look on his face
tells her everything.

His eyes grow wide as he edits a
groggy response. Stares at a
point just beyond her cheek.
Says he isn't there yet.
Not in love.

Despite disappointment, she savors
his unsettling. Watches as
he toads the slippery moment
and hunches low to conquer
the instinct to leap.

Barb Lundy

CONVERSION CHART

Use spice to induce appetite.
Pick habanero over jalapeno to ignite
mace instead of nutmeg to seduce.

Know the power of a pinch
the duration of a dash.
Fold scent into sustenance
to forge affinity.
Everything added endures.

Season to preserve
to tempt
to mask the mundane
to cultivate desire
to tease a tension that
eludes hunger.

BEFORE THE FROST

Hindu lotus span the north end of the pond and
goldfish congregate under their wide leaves.
Early September runs the high fever of July.

She lifts out aqua azolla and parrot feathers.
Sets them in the washtub with blue flag iris.
All to wait out winter in the potting shed.

Behind the waterfall, honeysuckle stretches the
lattice wall where a border of forget-me-nots
crowd the lavender petals of mourning brides.

The water lilies remain year round. Sink deep below
the liquid surface when winds chill. She envies
months of drifting in slow and silent water.

Aches to retreat from expectation. To
delay demands until a spring sun stirs
buried inspiration in her bones.

Barb Lundy

THE MASTERMIND

At the alternative energy rally
he leaned over and asked
        If you struck a match in a room filled
        with methane gas, what would happen?
Nothing, she said
without some oxygen.

When they dated she watched his riddles
rattle the best minds
        Tally the dirt in a ditch 2.6 meters
deep and 3.7 meters wide.
As soon as he got a number, he'd point out
that a ditch doesn't have dirt in it.

After a few months of marriage she
began to weigh his words with care.
        You act like water at 32 degrees
        that weighs less solid than liquid.
She translated in silence.
He'd just called her an ice queen.

Weeks later she posed this question. If a man tolerates
10 snubs, will he endure another?
        The odds are good, he said.
        It's conditioning.
Wrong, she corrected, handing him divorce papers.
Probability holds at 50/50.

THE DISAPPEARANCE

If time travels in the Hopi way
where midnight and first light stay
coiled into air alive with fey
where dreams fly past the sleeping eye
fill with dust and fleeting rain from skies
that settle into hum and fireflies
then endless space stretches up and stretches wide
swells to the imagined, the untried
that seconds, minutes, hours can divide.
And if the past no longer stays behind
no longer seeks to badger and remind
and day becomes amorphous, unconfined
would our feet fit firm against the ground?
The green scent of morning and the sound
of eager thrush and early breeze abound.
A ripe peach and a cup of tea
a corn muffin lightly spread with ghee
and nothing to remember or foresee.

Four

"It is what you don't write that frequently gives what you do write its power."

-Toni Morrison

A CAUTION

Watch out for the hollow spaces
no one can see,
spaces covered with the thin plastic of
deadlines and dinner dates.

No one can see
the times between
deadlines and dinner dates
when you bury fresh dreads.

In those times between
you navigate a minefield of doubt
because when you bury fresh dreads
you forget to mark the places.

You navigate this minefield of doubt
of uncertainty, of suspicions
of forgotten, unmarked places
until all feeling festers below the skin.

Marie Bracquemond's

THE LADY IN WHITE: CA 1880

I paint predictions of a nearing dark into her eyes
    vision tunneled by
    the fatigue
    of acute recognition.

My husband once praised my work
    I exacted precise patterns
    and detailed niches
    at brush tip.

Because her gaze relumes a dissident knowing
    because sunlight sheers
    the folds and frills
    of her summer gown

He disapproves. I know I have
    frightened him. I exile
    sights that ache
    for a silking of oils.

Barb Lundy

FACETS

Her reticent mother and professorial
father explored jewel names
like Opal, Jade and Topaz.
They agreed, finally, on Ruby.

Ruby required deep dolcetto eyes
a jazz-rhythm walk,
literary passions.

Their illusions ebbed. They tagged
her Sunny by two. She changed
her name officially in high school and
soon after married a
guy named Gilbert.

A TAXING SYLLOGISM

All people need to learn
to examine and to muse
to test possibilities
to investigate interests

Colleges are higher learning centers
that assemble uniform information
that promote answers not questions
that certify completion not mastery

Therefore, all people who attend college learn
how to attract dollars with degrees
how to anticipate the expected
how to evade original thinking.

Barb Lundy

NORA

Dew clings to damask petals turned out to
the sun. She does not use gloves to prune.
The roses indulge her. Twisting, may God be
her witness, to keep spike studded stems
from piercing her attentive hands.

The roses sense only tranquility, cannot feel the
calloused skin contoured by years of cleaning
other people's houses, cooking other people's meals.
Every Sunday grandchildren's legs dangle
from covered couches and she worries

their heels will mar unprotected carved oak trim.
She offers them 7-UP in gold rimmed glasses
with a candied cherry, like those she once served
from other people's silver trays. The children
take each glass, but shrink from her.

She hears them whispering as she leaves. The roses
whisper too in the early afternoon breezes. And she
hums snatches of minor key lullabies as she trims.
Songs sung to other people's children.
She never sang to her own.

ACCIDENTAL ALCHEMY

Had her grandfather packed the
dishes and cups with
something more than
old newspapers, the heirlooms

might have survived.
Jagged pieces of gilt gold
of painted rose, of silver
vines and clear crushed crystal
suggest contours and patterns.

Splinters seam aureate skirts
shards form a mosaic of harps
fragments swirl to tiffany fans.
Dancers dash on sliver-glass slippers.

Barb Lundy

AT THE ROAD SHOW

You have a marvelous piece done
quite near the end of her life.
Clean lines form an abstract of late
season leaves that fade from apricot to
jasmine then spill to intense ambers.

When I hold the vase near the light you can see
fragile patterns merge in a sheer, very nearly
brittle glass overlay. She quit the
states in her 60s for a town outside of
Paris and began experimenting.

She infused layers of color with movement.
One wonders if she flung a molten mesh into wind.
A splendid museum find, though she
insisted her created art for use. Fill it with
fresh cut flowers after you appraise. Insure.

IMMUTABLE

Thousands of years of glacier defrosted
                                        The Roman Marcellus kept at it
not far from Denver
                                        until he conquered Syracuse
revealing an ice age wooly mammoth
                                        ordering destruction to all but Archimedes.
carcass reclining in slush.
          The old mathematician, engrossed in making circles in dust
The big find made big news
                                        ignored a command to come along
so no one listened to the guy
                                        and the enraged conscript thrust his sword
for kill
who asked why everything was melting.
          leaving the problem unsolved.

Barb Lundy

COMMAS

Plum, azure and gold
blur as she spins in front of him.
I love paisley commas, the most
telling truths poise on the pause.

Reaching for her hand, he draws her
to him. She sinks into the comfort,
nods when he asks
but is it a wedding dress?

On the walk to the Magistrate's she tries
to remember who, between Budapest
and London, suggested marriage.
Each coupled step confirms agreement.

They exchange staccato I do's. Turn to seal the
promise. Fleeting distraction splits his gaze.
Hesitation lingers on his dry lips just as
they reach her own. She pretends not to see.

ROOTED

I agreed to stay for one
season of forsythia
to push a strong finger
through weathered bark
to drink iced rain until
wild bell wings perched
canary yellow on swaying
lissome branches.

I agreed to stay until the
last of my petals
gave way to greening
gave way to leaves spined
to withstand summer lightning
and long October chills.

I can't remember how
grief transformed to an eerie
knowing. A secret longing
whenever someone dies.

Barb Lundy

ADVISORY

When thunder resonates
in your fingertips
when electric white veins
charge the air
act before the storm arrives.

Open every window
to let lightning sweep the space
cover every mirror
to keep the power
flowing in one direction.

This ancient prescription
can ward off danger
or invite possibility.
Take the same steps for both.
Intent is everything.

SCARLET OAKS AT TURNING

In that hour when fireflies began to
Flicker, our first secrets burned on
our lips for telling. We hint to others
what we dared not ask ourselves.

How different the confidences of masquerade
years. The discovery of invisible and
unwanted truths. Whispered between us,
the shared silences seeped to slow spoil.

We embrace freedom late. Scatter
wasted fears on unkempt days.
Walk the way of spiral winds.
Attempt our own unriddling.

Barb Lundy

THE LAST SPEAKER

Say Black Hawk Lake and mean a place.

She brings night fire scents alive.
Each syllable steeped in dread and daring.

Say yesterday and mean many days past.

She pronounces a dawn to dusk protest
that leaves legs too tired to rest.

Say Rising Crow and mean a lover.

She gasps for air against genocide
and transcribes years of loss.

Say fire wheel and mean a wildflower.

She speaks in drum and flute.
And dancers leap alive in fields beneath the hills.

Say memory and mean forgotten sounds.

No one repeats the old words.
She mourns the language that dies with her.

HAT TRICKS

At the edge of winter, while the snake still sleeps
I will tell you the story of The Listener. When his
hair flows free his heart speaks his every word.
Eyes spark a galaxy of stars that circle his head.
But watch. On certain days he glosses his hair

pulls it skull-tight into a ringed tail. Pulls song
and stars close. Other days, when hungry eyes
search his, he ties on a red bandanna
and knots it hard behind the tail. That way
few can catch his thoughts as he passes.

On crowded days he tops his glossed
bandannaed head with his high felt hat.
Takes refuge beneath its rim. Hums his center quiet.
He does not know that the gifts of forgotten fathers
fill his veins. Like the snake, instinct foretells

his movement. He does not know his ancient eye
reads heart words, awakens soul stars invisible
to others. He does not know his ritual hat tricks
can trick him. He does not know that
to listen The Listener sets his hair free.

Barb Lundy

SONG WOMAN

At the azure lake she sees hawks glide on air.
Relives the slow descent down mountain sides
and the windburn of the sun when her brother died.
At water's edge she sings walking months despair
then twines fresh sage with cedar needle leaves
and burns the stick until smoke curls long
and the beating of her hand sounds out from song.
One day her face appears on the story tree.
They say her chants drive out desert droughts
ward off floods and conjure spirit cures
so everyone repeats then learns her words
though she never wished to shape their thoughts.
Decades after death they call her guide,
the small song woman that they deified.

ORIENTATION

The key is having few insights.
Take some notes and nod your head
until you figure who's in tight.

Then with some changes, very slight
repeat with vigor what's been said.
The key is having few insights.

Know very little going in
a condition that is quite widespread
until you figure who's in tight.

If you have to speak, keep it trite
and train your eyes on the overhead.
The key is having few insights.

Take special note of meeting rites
then memorize what's left unsaid
until you figure who's in tight.

And once you see who's got it right
you'll know just how to get ahead.
The key is having few insights
until you figure who's in tight.

Barb Lundy

EDDY STREET

The aunts interrogate at Sunday
dinner. They circle the table
topped with a plywood plank
to fit in husbands and children.
It takes two second best linens
to cover the distance.

Will you have another slice of turkey?
Take a Parker House roll before
they get cold. Did you see we have
two wakes this Tuesday? And
All Saints is as far as you can get
from Our Lady of Angels.

They retreat with leftovers. Questions
simmer above soaking rose china and
the rip of cheesecloth sized to wrap
cloved ham. Can you imagine? Won't
tongues fly now. And what about
those McGillicuddy sisters?

What kind of woman wants
to be a judge? Those Your Honors
never lifting a finger to help.
No man'll have them.
Then again, they might just
have the ticket.

Acknowledgements

Thanks to Jane and Carl Bock for prodding me to complete this. Special thanks to readers, Shirley Adler, Lucinda Borchard, Helen Buchanan and Barbara Nichols

Grateful acknowledgement to editors of the publications in which many poems in this book, or earlier versions of them, first appeared. Amarillo Bay, Art Times, The Baltimore Review, Blue Unicorn, California Quarterly, Carte Blanche Literary Magazine, Chaffey Review, Chaffin Journal, Cider Press Review, Connecticut River Review, Cumberland Poetry Review, Earth's Daughters, Emprise Review, Flutter Poetry Journal, Fox Cry Review, Green Hills Literary Lantern, Hawaii Pacific Review, Harp Strings Poetry Journal, Iconoclast, International Poetry Review, Licking River Review, Lilliput Review, Little Brown, Lullwater Review, Mad Poets Review, Main Street Rag, Mid-America Poetry Review, Miranda Literary Magazine, Mobius Literary Journal, Northeast, Pegasus, Plainsongs, Poem, Poetry Depth Quarterly, Poetry Harbor, Poetry Motel, Potomac Review, Rattle, Slant, SubtleTea.com, Tertulia Magazine, The Cape Rock, The Chaffin Journal, The Greensilk Journal, The Journal of the American Medical Association, The Lyric, The MacGuffin, Wazee Journal, Weber Studies, Westview, Whetstone, Xanadu.

Thank you for reading.
Please review this book. Reviews
help others find Absolutely Amazing eBooks and
inspire us to keep providing these marvelous tales.
If you would like to be put on our email list
to receive updates on new releases,
contests, and promotions, please go to
AbsolutelyAmazingEbooks.com and sign up.

About the Author

Barb Lundy grew up in a family of visual artists and writers. Legally blind until she turned 8, reading became a cherished pastime. Her parents gave her a subscription for The Writer magazine at her 12th birthday and her older brother gave her a used Royal Typewriter. So the ink was set. Barb had the good fortune to share a close friendship with award-winning poet Lois Beebe Hayna. Lois provided unvarnished critique.

A widely published poet, Lundy is listed in the Directory of Poets and Writers. She taught writing in Denver area colleges and is the current co-president of Colorado Authors League.

The Fiction of Stone

Barb Lundy

The New Atlantian Library

Made in the USA
Coppell, TX
16 December 2020

45352708R00059